NOVELTY CAKES

Consultant Editor:
Valerie Ferguson

HERMES
HOUSE

Contents

Introduction

A home-made cake is a lovely way
to show that you care, but there is
nothing so special as one designed
uniquely for the occasion. A novelty
cake is a wonderful way to celebrate
a special event or birthday and can
provide an amusing twist to traditional
occasions. In the following pages, there
are original cake designs for people of
all ages, unusual cakes for special
occasions and seasonal celebrations,
and fantasy cakes for fun at any time.

For the kids there are cakes shaped
like animals, a mermaid and even a
pizza, while for adults, there are
designs to reflect hobbies and interests,
from an artist's palette to a blooming
flowerpot. Celebrate special occasions,
from Mother's Day to Hallowe'en,
with an appropriate cake to add the
finishing touch.

The cakes are all highly distinctive,
but not too difficult to achieve. All are
made from basic cake recipes, icings
and glazes, and step-by-step
instructions for these form the first
chapter of this book.

You can follow the projects exactly
or adapt techniques to suit your own
family events. Whether you want to
celebrate Christmas, a birthday or
simply say "thank you", do it in style
with a novelty cake.

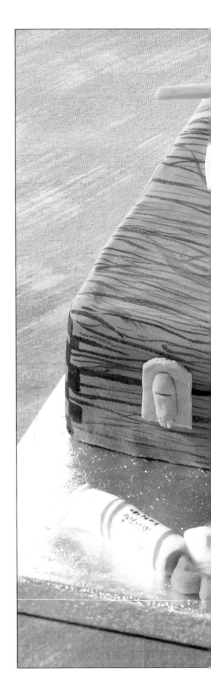

Equipment

To obtain the best results when making cakes, it is necessary to have a selection of good equipment.

A selection of useful items for cake making and decorating.

• Accurate weighing scales, measuring spoons and jugs are available in both metric and imperial measurements. Always measure level when using spoons unless otherwise stated in the recipe.

• A set of mixing bowls in various sizes and a selection of wooden spoons are essential items. However, an electric hand–held beater will save time and make cake-making easier.

• Cake tins; the most regularly used are round or square in sizes 15 cm/6 in, 20 cm/8 in and 25 cm/10 in.

• Cooling racks; at least two racks are useful for cake making and decorating.

• A serrated knife for cutting the cooled cake without it crumbling.

• Pastry brush for brushing cakes with apricot glaze.

• A heavy rolling pin for rolling out marzipan and sugarpaste icing.

• Pastry and small biscuit cutters in various shapes and sizes for cutting sugarpaste icing shapes.

• A palette knife for spreading

• Piping bags and a variety of nozzles (or you can use greaseproof paper cones with the nozzles).

• A turntable is not essential but makes icing much easier.

• Sable paintbrushes for painting fine details on to cakes.

• Silver cake boards for presenting decorated cakes.

Successful Cake Making

here are a few simple guidelines which must be followed to achieve the
st results when making any cake.

Always use the correct shape and size
tin for the recipe and make sure the
is properly prepared and lined.
Check that you have all the necessary
gredients measured correctly and that
ey are at the right temperature before
u start mixing.
Ensure soft margarine is kept chilled
the fridge to maintain the right
nsistency. Leave butter out to reach
om temperature.
Sift all dry ingredients to help aerate
e mixture and to disperse lumps.
Use the correct sugar. Caster sugar
eams more easily with fats than
anulated sugar, and is used where a
ne and soft texture is required. Soft
own sugar is used for some recipes
hen making heavier cakes.
Use good quality fruit and peel for
uit cake recipes. Sometimes stored
ltanas can become hard.
When making cakes by hand, beat
ell with a wooden spoon until the
ixture is light and glossy; scrape
own the mixture from the sides of
e bowl during beating with a plastic
ixing spatula to ensure even mixing.
f a cake is being made in a food
ocessor or an electric mixer, be very
reful not to overprocess or overbeat.
rape down the batter with a plastic
atula during mixing.

• If ingredients have to be folded into
a mixture, use a plastic spatula with a
flexible blade.
• Level cake mixtures before baking.
• Check that your oven is preheated to
the temperature stated in the recipe.
Failure to do so will affect the rising
of the cake and the cooking time.
• If the cake appears to be cooked
before the given time, it may indicate
that the oven is too hot; conversely, if
it takes longer to cook, it means the
oven is too cool.
• The temperature of the cake mixture
can cause the cooking time to vary. If
conditions are cold, the mixture will
be cold and take longer to cook and if
it is warm the cooking time will be
slightly quicker.
• The surface of the cake should be
evenly browned and level; if the cake is
overcooked or risen to one side, then
the heat in the oven is uneven or the
oven shelf is not level.

Techniques

Lining a Shallow Cake Tin

Lining tins is important so that the cake comes out of the tin without breaking or sticking to the base of the tin. This method is simple, but essential.

1 Place the tin on a piece of greaseproof paper, draw around the base with a pencil and cut out the paper inside this line to fit tightly.

2 Grease the base and side of the tin with melted lard or soft margarine. Grease the paper and then place it neatly into the tin. It is now ready for filling with the cake mixture.

3 To line the sides of a tin: Cut a strip of paper long enough to wrap around the outside of the tin and overlap by 4 cm/1½ in. It should be wider than the depth of the tin by 2.5 cm/1 in.

4 Fold the strip lengthways at the 2.5 cm/1 in point and crease. Snip at regular intervals from the edge to the crease along the fold. Line the side of the tin, with the snipped part of the strip on and overlapping the base. Pre the bottom lining in (Steps 1 and 2).

5 For square and rectangular cake tins, fold the paper and crease it with your fingernail to fit snugly into the corners of the tin. Then press the bottom paper lining into place.

ining a Deep Cake Tin

Place the tin on a double thickness
greaseproof paper or baking
rchment. Draw around the base with
pencil. Cut out the marked shape
ith a pair of scissors.

Cut a strip of double-thickness
easeproof paper or baking parchment
ng enough to wrap around the
itside of the tin, leaving a small
erlap. It should stand 2.5cm/1in
ove the top of the tin.

Brush the base and side of the tin
ith melted vegetable fat or oil. Place
e double strip of paper inside the tin,
essing well against the sides and
aking sharp creases if it must fit into
orners. Place the cut-out shape in the
ase of the tin and press it flat.

Brush the base and side papers well
ith melted vegetable fat or oil. Place
strip of double-thickness brown
aper around the outside of the tin
nd tie securely with a string.

Line a baking sheet with three or
our layers of brown paper and stand
e tin on top.

Preparing Cake Tins

Instructions vary for preparing cake
tins, depending on the mixture and the
baking time. Proper preparation aids
turning out.

1 To grease a tin: If using butter or
margarine, hold a small piece in
kitchen paper (or use your fingers),
and rub it all over the base and side of
the tin to make a thin, even coating.
If using oil, brush a small amount on
with a pastry brush.

2 To flour a tin: Put a small scoop of
flour in the centre of the greased tin.
Tip and rotate the tin to coat the base
and side. Shake out excess flour,
tapping to dislodge any pockets.

Quick-mix Sponge Cake

Choose chocolate, lemon or orange flavouring for this light and versatile sponge cake, or leave it plain.

Makes 1 x 20 cm/8 in round or 18 cm/7 in square cake

INGREDIENTS
115 g/4 oz/1 cup self-raising flour
5 ml/1 tsp baking powder
115 g/4 oz/8 tbsp soft margarine
115 g/4 oz/generous ½ cup caster sugar
2 eggs

FOR THE FLAVOURINGS
Chocolate: 15 ml/1 tbsp cocoa powder
    blended with 15 ml/1 tbsp boiling water
Lemon: 10 ml/2 tsp grated lemon rind
Orange: 15 ml/1 tbsp grated orange rind

1 Preheat the oven to 160°C/325°F/ Gas 3. Grease and line a 20 cm/8 in round tin or 18 cm/7 in square tin.

2 Sift the flour and baking powder into a bowl. Add the margarine, sugar and eggs with the chosen flavourings if using.

3 Beat with a wooden spoon for 2– minutes. The mixture should be pale in colour and slightly glossy.

4 Spoon the mixture into the cake tin and smooth the surface. Bake in the centre of the oven for 30–40 minutes, or until a skewer inserted in the centre of the cake comes out clean. Turn out on to a wire rack, remove the lining paper and leave to cool completely.

Madeira Cake

This is a richer basic cake which is ideal for decorating.

Makes 1 x 20 cm round or
18 cm/7 in square cake

INGREDIENTS
275 g/8 oz/2 cups plain flour
5 ml/1 tsp baking powder
225 g/8 oz/1 cup butter or margarine,
at room temperature
225 g/8 oz/generous 1 cup caster sugar
grated rind of 1 lemon
5 ml/1 tsp vanilla essence
3 eggs

1 Preheat the oven to 160°C/325°F/
Gas 3. Grease and line a cake tin.

2 Sift the flour and baking powder
into a bowl. Set the mixture aside.

3 Cream the butter or margarine,
adding the caster sugar about 30 ml/
2 tbsp at a time, until light and fluffy.
Stir in the lemon rind and vanilla
essence. Add the eggs, one at a time,
beating for 1 minute after each
addition. Add the flour mixture and
stir until just combined.

4 Pour the cake mixture into the
prepared tin and tap lightly to level.
Bake for about 1¼ hours, or until a
metal skewer inserted in the centre
comes out clean.

5 Cool in the tin on a wire rack for
10 minutes, then turn the cake out
and leave to cool completely.

Rich Fruit Cake

Make this cake a few weeks before icing, wrap well and store in an airtight container to mature.

Makes 1 x 20 cm/8 in round or 18 cm/7 in square cake

INGREDIENTS
375 g/13 oz/1¾ cups currants
250 g/9 oz/1½ cups sultanas
150 g/5 oz/1 cup raisins
90 g/3½ oz/scant ½ cup glacé
    cherries, halved
90 g/3½ oz/scant 1 cup almonds, chopped
65 g/2½ oz/scant ½ cup mixed peel
grated rind of 1 lemon
40 ml/2½ tbsp brandy
250 g/9 oz/2¼ cups plain flour, sifted
6.5 ml/1¼ tsp mixed spice
2.5 ml/½ tsp grated nutmeg
65 g/2½ oz/generous ½ cup ground almonds
200 g/7 oz/scant 1 cup soft margarine
    or butter
225 g/8 oz/1 cup soft brown sugar
15 ml/1 tbsp black treacle
5 eggs, beaten

1 Preheat the oven to 140°C/275°F/ Gas 1. Grease and line the base and sides of a 20 cm/8 in round cake tin or an 18 cm/7 in square cake tin with a double thickness of greaseproof paper.

2 Combine the ingredients in a large mixing bowl. Beat with a wooden spoon for 5 minutes. Spoon the mixture into the prepared tin. Make a slight depression in the centre.

3 Bake in the centre of the oven for 3–3½ hours. Test the cake after 3 hours. If it is ready it will feel firm, and a skewer inserted in the centre will come out clean. Cover the top loosely with foil if it starts to brown too quickly.

4 Leave to cool completely in the tin, then turn out. The lining paper can be left on to keep the cake moist.

Butter Icing

he creamy rich flavour and silky smoothness of butter icing is popular
ith both children and adults.

Makes 350 g/12 oz/1½ cups

INGREDIENTS

25 g/8 oz/2 cups icing
sugar, sifted
5 g/3 oz/6 tbsp soft margarine or
butter, softened
ml/1 tsp vanilla essence
0–15 ml/2–3 tsp milk

OR THE FLAVOURINGS

Chocolate: Blend 15 ml/1 tbsp cocoa powder
with 15 ml/1 tbsp hot water. Cool before
beating into the icing.

Coffee: Blend 10 ml/2 tsp coffee powder
with 15 ml/1 tbsp boiling water. Omit the
milk. Cool before beating the mixture into
the icing.

Lemon, orange or lime: Replace the vanilla
essence and milk with lemon, orange or
lime juice and 10 ml/2 tsp finely grated
citrus rind. Omit the rind if using the icing
for piping. Lightly tint the icing with food
colouring, if wished.

COOK'S TIP: Use Butter Icing for
fillings, toppings and as a thin
coating over a cake before adding
Sugarpaste Icing.
    The icing will keep for up to
3 days in an airtight container stored
in the fridge.

1 Put the icing sugar, margarine or
butter, vanilla essence and 5 ml/1 tsp
of the milk into a bowl.

2 Beat with a wooden spoon or an
electric mixer until creamy. Add
sufficient extra milk, a little at a time
until the icing has a light, smooth and
fluffy consistency.

3 To make flavoured butter icing,
follow the instructions for chocolate,
coffee or citrus flavourings given above
for the flavour of your choice.

Marzipan

This is very versatile and can be used on its own, under an icing or for modelling.

Makes 450 g/1 lb/3 cups

INGREDIENTS
225 g/8 oz/2 cups ground almonds
115 g/4 oz/generous ½ cup caster sugar
115 g/4 oz/1 cup icing sugar, sifted
5 ml/1 tsp lemon juice
a few drops of almond essence
1 small egg, or 1 medium egg white
food colouring (optional)

1 Stir the ground almonds and caster and icing sugars together in a bowl until evenly mixed. Make a well in the centre and add the lemon juice, almond essence and enough egg or egg white to mix to a soft, but firm dough, using a wooden spoon.

2 Form the marzipan into a ball. Lightly dust a surface with icing sugar and knead the marzipan until smooth. Wrap in clear film or store in a polythene bag until needed. Tint with food colouring if required.

Sugarpaste Icing

This icing is wonderfully pliab and can be coloured, moulded and shaped.

Makes 350 g/12 oz/2¼ cup

INGREDIENTS
1 egg white
15 ml/1 tbsp liquid glucose, warmed
350 g/12 oz/3 cups icing
    sugar, sifted

1 Put the egg white and glucose mixing bowl. Stir them together t break up the egg white. Add the i sugar and mix together with a pa] knife, using a chopping action, un well blended and the icing begins bind together. Knead the mixture your fingers until it forms a ball.

2 Knead the sugarpaste on a wo surface lightly dusted with icing s for several minutes until smooth, and pliable. If the icing is too soft knead in some more sifted sugar it reaches the right consistency.

Royal Icing

Use for a truly professional finish. This recipe makes enough icing to cover the top and sides of an 18 cm/7 in cake.

Makes 675 g/1½ lb/4½ cups

INGREDIENTS
3 egg whites
about 675 g/1½ lb/6 cups icing sugar, sifted
7.5 ml/½ tsp glycerine
a few drops of lemon juice
food colouring (optional)

2 Gradually add the icing sugar, beating well with a wooden spoon after each addition. Add enough icing sugar to make a smooth, shiny icing that has the consistency of very stiff meringue. Do not use an electric mixer as this will make the icing too fluffy.

1 Put the egg whites in a bowl and stir lightly with a fork or a wooden spoon to break them up.

COOK'S TIP: This recipe is for an icing consistency suitable for flat icing a marzipanned rich fruit cake. When the spoon is lifted, the icing should form a sharp point, with a slight curve at the end, known as "soft peak".

For piping, the icing needs to be slightly stiffer. It should form a fine sharp peak when the spoon is lifted. Add more icing sugar to achieve this consistency.

3 Beat in the glycerine, lemon juice and food colouring, if using. Leave for 1 hour, or up to 24 hours before using, covered with damp clear film, then stir to burst any air bubbles.

Apricot Glaze

Use the glaze to brush cakes before applying marzipan, or use for glazing fruits on gâteaux and cakes.

Makes 450 g/1 lb/1½ cups

INGREDIENTS
450 g/1 lb/1½ cups apricot jam
45 ml/3 tbsp water

1 Place the jam and water in a pan. Heat gently, stirring occasionally until melted. Boil rapidly for 1 minute.

2 Remove from the heat and rub through a sieve, pressing the fruit against the sides of the sieve with the back of a wooden spoon. Discard the skins left in the sieve.

3 Use a pastry brush to cover the entire surface of the cake.

Sugar-frosted Flowers

These pretty edible flowers may be used when a dainty and elegant decoration is required for a cake.

To cover about 20 flowers.

INGREDIENTS
Edible flowers, such as pansies,
    primroses, violets, roses, freesias
    or nasturtiums
1 egg white
caster sugar

1 Trim the stems from the flowers leaving approximately 2 cm/¾ in if possible. Wash the flowers and dry gently on kitchen paper. Lightly beat the egg white in a small bowl and sprinkle some caster sugar onto a plate. Line another plate with kitchen paper.

2 Using a paintbrush, evenly brush both sides of the petals with the egg white. Holding the flower by the stem over the paper-lined plate, sprinkle it evenly with the sugar and shake off any excess.

3 Place on a flat board or wire rack covered with kitchen paper and leave to dry in a warm place.

COOK'S TIP: The flower stems are kept long for frosting so that they are easy to hold. They can be trimmed afterwards, if preferred.

The Beautiful Present Cake

For a best friend, mother, grandmother, aunt or sister, this beautiful cake can mark any special occasion.

Serves 15–20

INGREDIENTS
2 x quantity Quick-mix Sponge Cake, baked
    in a 23 cm/9 in square cake tin
1 quantity Butter Icing
60 ml/4 tbsp Apricot Glaze
1¼ x quantity Marzipan
1⅔ x quantity Sugarpaste Icing
purple and pink food colouring and pen

1 Cut the cake in half horizontally. sandwich the halves together with butter icing, place on a cake board and brush with apricot glaze. Roll out the marzipan on a surface lightly dusted with icing sugar to about 5 mm/¼ in thickness and use to cover the cake.

2 Colour about five-eighths of the sugarpaste purple. Roll out on a lightly dusted surface and use to cover the cake. With a heart-shape biscuit cutter, stamp out a pattern from the icing. Remove the hearts with a knife, knead, wrap in clear film and reserve.

3 Colour the remaining icing pink and roll out to a 5 mm/¼ in thickness. Cut out hearts to fill the spaces. Wrap the trimmings and reserve.

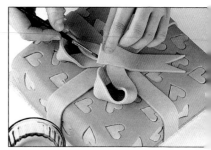

4 Roll out the pink icing and cut into three strips 2 cm/¾ in wide and 30 cm/12 in long. Lay two at right angles across the centre of cake, brushing with a little water to secure. Reserve the trimmings. Divide the remaining strip into quarters and arrange in the centre of the cake to make a bow. Secure with a little water and reserve the trimmings.

5 Roll out all the remaining icing and cut two rounds of each colour with a small fluted cutter. Roll the edges with a cocktail stick to make frilled petals. Make two small purple balls for flower centres. Assemble the flowers and secure to the cake with a little water. Make a name tag from the trimmings. Write the name with a food–colouring pen and secure to the cake.

19

Terracotta Flowerpot

Ideal for celebrating a gardener's birthday or Mother's Day, this flowerpot cake is filled with a colourful arrangement of icing flowers and foliage.

Serves 15

INGREDIENTS
1 x quantity Madeira Cake, baked in a
   1.2 litre/2 pint/5 cup pudding basin
175 g/6 oz/generous ½ cup jam
½ x quantity Butter Icing
30 ml/2 tbsp Apricot Glaze
2 x quantity Sugarpaste Icing
orange-red, red, silver, green, purple and
   yellow food colouring
2 chocolate flakes, crushed
2 x quantity Royal Icing

1 Slice the cake into three layers and stick together with jam and butter icing. Cut out a shallow circle from the cake top, leaving a 1 cm/½ in rim.

2 Brush the outside of the cake and rim with apricot glaze. Tint 400 g/ 14 oz/2½ cups of the sugarpaste dark orange-red and cover the cake and rim. Reserve the trimmings. Leave to dry.

3 Use the trimmings to make decorations and handles for the flowerpot. Leave to dry on greaseproof paper before attaching using a little water. Sprinkle the chocolate flakes into the pot for soil.

4 Tint a small piece of sugarpaste very pale orange-red. Use to make a seed bag. When dry, paint on a pattern in food colouring. Tint two small pieces of icing red and silver. Make a trowel and leave to dry over a wooden spoon handle.

5 Tint the remaining icing green, purple and a small piece yellow. Use to make the flowers and leaves, attaching together with royal icing. Score leaf veins with the back of a knife. Make grass and seeds from trimmings. Leave to dry on greaseproof paper.

6 Place the leaves and flowers in the flowerpot with the seed bag, trowel, seeds and grass arranged around it.

Sun Cake

Whatever the star sign of the month, this cheerful sun cake would be a bright way to celebrate anyone's birthday.

Serves 10–12

INGREDIENTS
2 x quantity Quick-mix Sponge Cake,
   baked in 2 x 20 cm/8 in round tins
25 g/1 oz/2 tbsp unsalted butter
450 g/1 lb/4 cups sifted
   icing sugar
120 ml/4 fl oz/½ cup Apricot Glaze
2 large egg whites
1–2 drops glycerine
juice of 1 lemon
30 ml/2 tbsp water
yellow and orange
   food colouring

2 Brush the warm apricot glaze over the cake.

1 For the sunbeams cut one of the cakes into eight equal wedges. Cut away a rounded piece from the base of each so that they fit neatly up against the sides of the whole cake. Make butter icing with the butter and 25 g/ 1 oz/2 tbsp of the icing sugar. Place the whole cake on a 40 cm/16 in board and attach the sunbeams with the butter icing.

3 For the icing, beat the egg whites until stiff. Gradually add the icing sugar, glycerine and lemon juice, and beat for 1 minute. Reserve a small amount of icing for decoration, then tint the remainder yellow and spread over the cake. Tint the reserved icing bright yellow and orange. Pipe the details on to the cake.

COOK'S TIP: The icing should be spreadable. If necessary, thin with water or add icing sugar to thicken.

A Basket of Strawberries

Quick and easy to make, a perfect surprise for a birthday. Don't be put off by the icing technique, it's much easier than it looks!

Serves 6–8

INGREDIENTS
1 x quantity Quick-mix Sponge Cake,
    baked in a 450 g/1 lb loaf tin
45 ml/3 tbsp Apricot Glaze
1½ x quantity Marzipan
1 x quantity chocolate-flavour
    Butter Icing
red food colouring
50 g/2 oz/¼ cup caster sugar
10 plastic strawberry stalks
30 cm/12 in thin red ribbon

1 Level the top of the cake and make it perfectly flat. Score a 5 mm/¼ in border around the edge and scoop out the inside to make a shallow hollow. Brush the sides and border edges of the cake with apricot glaze.

2 Roll out 275 g/10 oz/scant 2 cups of the marzipan, cut into rectangles and use to cover the sides of the cake, overlapping the borders. Press the edges together to seal.

3 Using a basketweave nozzle, pipe vertical lines of chocolate-flavour butter icing 2.5 cm/1 in apart all around the sides of the cake. Pipe short horizontal lines alternately crossing over and then stopping at the vertical lines to give a basketweave effect. Using a star nozzle, pipe a decorative line of icing around the top edge of the basket to finish.

4 Tint the remaining marzipan red and mould it into ten strawberry shapes. Roll the shapes in the caster sugar and press a plastic stalk into each top. Carefully arrange the strawberries in the 'basket'.

5 For the basket handle, fold 30 x 7.5 cm/12 x 3 in strip of foil into a thin strip and wind the ribbon around it to cover. Bend up the ends and then bend into a curve. Push the ends into the sides of the cake. Decorate with bows made from ribbon.

The Beehive

The perfect cake for an outdoors spring or summer party. Take the bees along separately on their wires and insert them into the cake at the picni

Serves 8–10

INGREDIENTS
2 x quantity Marzipan
icing sugar, for dusting
1 x quantity Quick-mix Sponge Cake, baked
    in a 900 ml/1½ pint/3¾ cup pudding basin
75 ml/5 tbsp Apricot Glaze
black food colouring
20 cm/8 in square of rice paper
25 g/1 oz Sugarpaste Icing
florist's wire covered in florist's tape

1 Cut off about 175 g/6 oz of marzipan and set aside, wrapped in clear film. Knead the remainder on a surface lightly dusted with icing sugar, then roll into a long, thin sausage shape. If it breaks, make more than one sausage. Place the cake, dome side up, on a cake board and brush with apricot glaze.

2 Starting at the back of the base, coil the marzipan sausage around the cake. Place any joins at the back.

3 With a small, sharp knife, cut an arched doorway at the front. Remove the cut-out section and cut away som of the cake to make a hollow.

4 To make six bees, halve the reserve marzipan and colour one half black. Set aside a cherry-sized ball of black marzipan, wrapped in clear film.

5 Divide the remaining marzipan in 12 small balls in each colour. To make a bee, pinch together two balls of eac colour, alternately placed. Secure with a little water, if necessary. Cut the ric paper into six pairs of wings and stick to the bees with water.

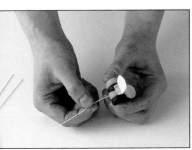

6 Use the reserved black marzipan and the sugarpaste icing to make the faces. Then cut the florist's wire into various lengths and pierce the bees from underneath. Once secure, press the other end of the wire into the cake. The wire must be removed before serving.

Mobile Phone Cake

For the upwardly mobile, this novel cake just has to be the business!

Serves 8–10

INGREDIENTS
1 x quantity Quick-mix Sponge Cake,
   baked in a 23 x 13 cm/9 x 5 in
   loaf tin
30 ml/2 tbsp Apricot Glaze
1 x quantity Sugarpaste Icing
black food colouring
10 small square sweets
30–45 ml/2–3 tbsp icing sugar
2.5–5 ml/½–1 tsp water

1 Turn the cake upside down. Make a 2.5 cm/1 in diagonal cut 2.5 cm/1 in from one end. Cut down vertically to remove the wedge. Remove the middle of the cake to the wedge depth up to 4 cm/1½ in from the other end.

2 Place the cake on a board and brush with apricot glaze. Tint 275 g/10 oz/1¾ cups of the sugarpaste icing black. Use to cover the cake, smoothing it over the carved shape. Reserve the trimmings.

3 Tint the remaining sugarpaste icing grey. Cut a piece to fit the hollowed centre, leaving a 1 cm/½ in border, and another piece 2.5 cm/1 in square. Stamp out the centre of the square with a diamond-shape cutter. Secure all the pieces on the cake with water.

4 Position the sweets and a small piece of foil for the display panel. For the glacé icing, mix the icing sugar with the water and tint black. With a small round nozzle, pipe border lines around the edges of the phone, including the grey pieces of sugarpaste. Pipe the numbers on the keys.

5 Roll a sausage shape from the reserved black sugarpaste for the aerial. Indent one side of the top with a knife and secure the aerial with water.

VARIATION: If preferred, use a little extra sugarpaste for the dial pad instead of the sweets.

Artist's Box & Palette

Making cakes is an art in itself, and this cake proves it. It is the perfect celebration cake for artists of all ages.

Serves 30

INGREDIENTS
1¼ x quantity Rich Fruit Cake, baked in a
    20 cm/8 in square tin
45 ml/3 tbsp Apricot Glaze
1 x quantity Marzipan
2⅓ x quantity Sugarpaste Icing
chestnut, yellow, blue, black, silver,
    paprika, green and mulberry
    food colouring
90 g/3½ oz/⅔ cup Royal Icing

1 Brush the cake with the apricot glaze. Cover in marzipan and leave to dry overnight.

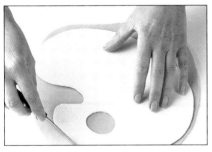

2 Make a template of a painter's palette that will fit the cake top. Tint 175 g/6 oz/generous 1 cup of the sugarpaste very pale chestnut. Cut out the palette shape from the tinted sugarpaste, place on greaseproof paper and leave to dry overnight.

3 Tint 450 g/1 lb/3 cups of the sugarpaste icing dark chestnut. Use to cover the cake. Secure the cake on a board with royal icing. Leave to dry.

4 Divide half the remaining sugarpaste icing into seven equal parts and tint yellow, blue, black, silver, paprika, green and mulberry. Make all the decorative pieces for the box and palette, using the remaining white sugarpaste for the paint tubes. Leave to dry on greaseproof paper.

5 Paint black markings on the paint tubes and chestnut wood markings on the box.

Position all the sugarpaste pieces on
e cake and board using royal icing.
ave to dry.

COOK'S TIP: Start modelling
the cake decorations the day
before assembling.

31

Glittering Star Cake

With a quick flick of a paintbrush you can give a sparkling effect to this glittering cake.

Serves 20–25

INGREDIENTS
1 x quantity Rich Fruit Cake, baked in a
    20 cm/8 in round tin
40 ml/2½ tbsp Apricot Glaze
1½ x quantity Marzipan
450 g/1 lb/3 cups Sugarpaste Icing
silver, gold, lilac shimmer, red sparkle, glitter
    green and primrose sparkle food colouring
    and powder tints
90 g/3½ oz/⅔ cup quantity Royal Icing

1 Brush the cake with the apricot glaze. Use two-thirds of the marzipan to cover the cake. Leave to dry overnight.

2 Cover the cake with the sugarpaste icing. Leave to dry.

3 Place the cake on a large sheet of greaseproof paper. Dilute a little powdered silver food colouring and, using a loaded paintbrush, flick it all over the cake to give a spattered effect. Allow to dry.

4 Make templates of two different-size moon shapes and three irregular star shapes. Divide the remaining marzipan into six pieces and tint silver, gold, lilac shimmer, red sparkle, glitter green and primrose. Using the templates, cut into stars and moons, cutting some of the stars in half.

5 Place the cut-outs on greaseproof paper, brush each with its own colou powder tint. Allow to dry.

6 Secure the cake on a board with royal icing. Arrange the stars and moons at different angles all over the cake, attaching with royal icing, and position the halved stars upright as though coming out of the cake. Allov to set.

COOK'S TIP: Stored in an airtight container, the cake will keep for up to 3 weeks.

Christening Sampler

Instead of embroidering a sampler to welcome a newborn baby, why no
make a sampler cake to celebrate?

Serves 30

INGREDIENTS
1¼ x quantity Rich Fruit Cake, baked in a
    20 cm/8 in square tin
45 ml/3 tbsp Apricot Glaze
1 x quantity Marzipan
2 x quantity Sugarpaste Icing
brown, yellow, orange, purple, cream, blue,
    green and pink food colouring

1 Brush the cake with apricot glaze.
Roll out the marzipan, cover the cake
and leave to dry overnight. Roll out
150 g/5 oz/1 cup of the sugarpaste
icing to fit the cake top. Brush the top
with water and cover with the icing.

2 Colour 300 g/11 oz/2 cups of the
icing brown and roll out four pieces to
the length and about 1 cm/½ in wider
than the cake sides. Brush the sides
with water and cover with icing,
folding over the extra width at the top
and cutting the corners at an angle to
make a frame. Place on a cake board.

3 With a fine paintbrush, paint fine
lines over the sides with watered-do
brown food colouring to represent
wood grain.

4 Take the remaining icing and colo
small amounts yellow, orange, brown
purple and cream and two shades of
blue, green and pink. Leave a little wh

5 Use these colours to shape the
ducks, teddy bear, bulrushes, water,
branch and leaves. Cut out a pink
heart with a biscuit cutter and make
the baby's initial from white icing. M
the white and pink icings together f
the apple blossom flowers.

6 Make the shapes for the border. Attach the decorations to the cake with a little water. Use the leftover colours to make "threads". Arrange in loops around the base of the cake on the cake board.

Valentine's Box of Chocolates

This special cake would also make a wonderful gift for Mother's Day.
Choose her favourite chocolates to go inside.

Serves 10–12

INGREDIENTS
1½ x quantity chocolate-flavour Quick-mix
    Sponge Cake, baked in a 20 cm/8 in
    heart-shaped tin
⅔ x quantity Marzipan
120 ml/4 fl oz/½ cup Apricot Glaze
3 x quantity Sugarpaste Icing
red food colouring
length of ribbon tied in a bow, and a pin
225 g/8 oz/about 16–20
    hand-made chocolates
small paper sweet cases

2 Roll the marzipan into a long
sausage to the measured length of th
string. Place on the cake around the
outside edge. Brush both sections of
the cake with apricot glaze. Tint the
sugarpaste icing red and cut off one-
third. Cut another 50 g/2 oz/⅓ cup
portion from the larger piece. Set
aside. Use the large piece to cover th
base section of cake.

1 Place the cake on a 23 cm/9 in
square piece of stiff card, draw around
it, and cut the heart shape out to make
a template. It will be used to support
the box lid. Using a sharp knife, cut
through the cake horizontally, just
below the dome. Place the top section
on the card and the base on a board.
Use a piece of string to measure
around the outside of the base.

3 Stand the lid on a raised surface.
Use the reserved one-third of
sugarpaste icing to cover the lid. Rol
out the remaining piece of icing and
stamp out small hearts with a biscuit
cutter. Stick them around the edge o
the lid with water. Secure the ribbor
bow on top of the lid with the pin.

4 Place the chocolates in the paper
cases and arrange in the cake base.
Position the lid slightly off-centre, to
reveal the chocolates. **Do not forge
to remove the ribbon and pin
before serving the cake.**

Lucky Horseshoe Cake

This horseshoe-shaped cake, made to wish "good luck", is made from a round cake cut to shape. Use a crimping tool for the edge.

Serves 30–35

INGREDIENTS
1½ x quantity Rich Fruit Cake, baked in a
    25 cm/10 in round tin
60 ml/4 tbsp Apricot Glaze
2 x quantity Marzipan
3 x quantity Sugarpaste Icing
peach and blue food colouring
3 mm/⅛ in wide blue ribbon
edible silver balls
90 g/3½ oz/⅔ cup Royal Icing

1 Make a horseshoe template and use to shape the cake. Brush the cake with apricot glaze. Cover the cake with marzipan using the template and 350 g/12 oz/2¼ cups of marzipan for the top, and measuring the inside and outside of the cake to cover with the remaining marzipan. Place on a board and leave overnight.

2 Tint 800 g/1¾ lb/5¼ cups of the sugarpaste icing peach. Cover the cake in the same way. Crimp the top edge.

3 Draw and measure the ribbon insertion on the template. Cut 13 pieces of ribbon fractionally longer than each slit. Make the slits in the icing through the template with a scalpel. Insert the ribbon with a pointed tool. Leave to dry overnight

4 Tint half the remaining sugarpaste icing pale blue. Cut out nine blue small horseshoe shapes. Mark each horseshoe with a sharp knife. Cut ou 12 large and 15 small blossoms with blossom cutters. Press a silver ball int the centres of the larger blossoms. D Repeat with the white icing. Decora the cake, securing with royal icing.

Mother's Day Basket

Every mother would love to receive a cake like this on Mother's Day.
Choose fresh flowers to decorate the top.

Serves 12

INGREDIENTS
1½ x quantity orange-flavour Quick-mix
Sponge Cake, baked in a fluted dish
or brioche mould
3 x quantity orange-flavour
Butter Icing
1 m/1 yd x 1 cm/½ in wide
mauve ribbon
50 cm/20 in x 3 mm/⅛ in wide spotted
mauve ribbon
fresh flowers

1 Spread the side of the cake with
one-third of the butter icing and place
upside down on a board.

2 Half fill a piping bag fitted with a
basketweave nozzle with butter icing.
Pipe a vertical line down the side of
the cake, then pipe four horizontal
lines across the vertical line, starting at
the top of the cake and equally spacing
the lines apart.

3 Pipe another vertical line of icing
on the edge of the horizontal lines,
then pipe four horizontal lines across
this between the spaces formed by the
previous horizontal lines, to form a
basket-weave. Continue in this way
until the side is completly covered.

4 Invert the cake on to the cake
board and spread the top with butter
icing. Pipe a shell edging, using the
basket-weave nozzle, to neaten the top
edge. Continue to pipe the basket-
weave icing across the top of the cake,
starting at the edge. Leave the cake to
set in a cool place.

5 Fold a piece of foil in half, then
again and continue to fold until you
have a strip several layers thick. Using
the 1 cm/½ in wide mauve ribbon,
bind the strip to cover the foil; bend
up the end to secure the ribbon. Bend
the foil to make a handle, and press
into the icing.

6 Choose some flowers and make a neat arrangement tied with the spotted ribbon on top of the cake just before serving. Tie a bow and pin it to the sides of the cake.

COOK'S TIP: Wrap the flower stalks in silver paper, if liked.

Double Heart Engagement Cake

For a celebratory party, these sumptuous cakes make the perfect centrepiece.

Serves 20

INGREDIENTS
350 g/12 oz plain chocolate
2 x quantity chocolate-flavour
   Quick-mix Sponge Cakes,
   baked in 20 cm/8 in
   heart-shaped tins
2 x quantity coffee-flavour
   Butter Icing
icing sugar, for dusting
fresh raspberries,
   to decorate

1 Melt the chocolate in a heatproof bowl over a saucepan of hot water (you may find it easier to work with half the chocolate at a time). Pour the chocolate on to a smooth, non-porous surface and spread it out with a palette knife. Leave to cool slightly until just set, but not hard.

2 To make the chocolate curls, hold a large sharp knife at a 45° angle to the chocolate and push it along the chocolate in short sawing movements. Leave to set on greaseproof paper.

COOK'S TIP: The finished cakes can be kept for up to 3 days in an airtight container in the fridge.

3 Cut each cake in half horizontally. Use one-third of the butter icing to sandwich the cakes together. Use the remaining icing to coat the tops and sides of the cakes.

4 Place the cakes on heart-shaped cake boards. Generously cover the tops and sides of the cakes with the chocolate curls, pressing them gently into the butter icing.

5 Sift a little icing sugar over the tops of each cake and decorate with raspberries. Chill until ready to serve.

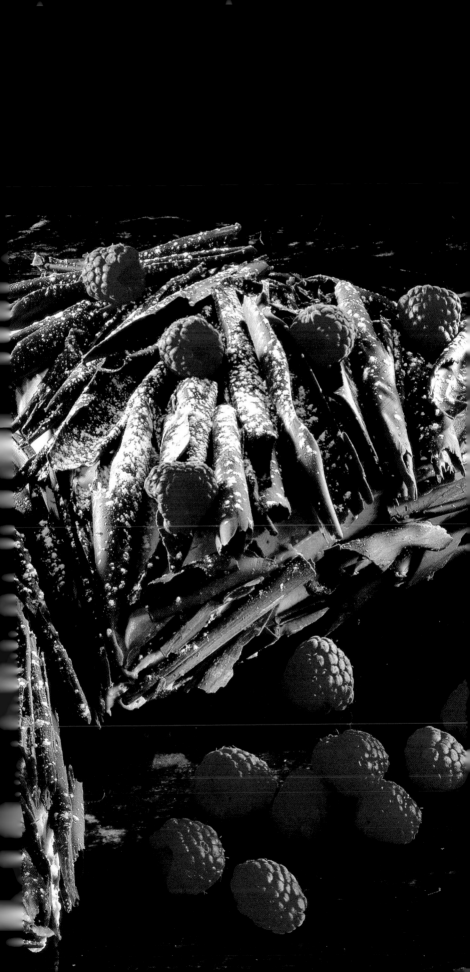

Hallowe'en Pumpkin

This is the time for spooky cakes, and witches may even burst out of them. Make the cake and butter icing your favourite flavour.

Serves 15

INGREDIENTS
1 x quantity Madeira Cake, baked in two
    1.2 litre/2 pint/5 cup pudding basins
1 x quantity orange-flavour Butter Icing
1½ x quantity Sugarpaste Icing
orange, black and yellow food colouring
90 g/3½ oz/⅔ cup Royal Icing

1 Trim the widest ends of the cakes so that they will fit together. Split each cake in half horizontally, then sandwich the layers together with butter icing. Trim one end narrower for a better shape and to form the base. Cover the cake with the remaining butter icing.

2 Colour 350 g/12 oz/2¼ cups of the sugarpaste icing orange. Roll out and cover the cake, trimming to fit. Reserve the trimmings. Mark segments on the icing with a skewer. Paint the markings of pumpkin flesh with watered-down orange food colouring.

3 Cut and tear the sugarpaste trimmings into jagged pieces, to make the place where the witch bursts out. Attach to the cake with a little water.

4 Colour three-quarters of the remaining sugarpaste icing black. Colour a little of the remainder yellow and leave the rest white. Use black and white icing to make the witch's head, arms and body, joining them with royal icing.

5 Make the cape and hat from black icing. Shape the cauldron, broomstick and cat's head from black and yellow icing, securing the cauldron handle with royal icing when dry. Leave to dry

6 Use a sharp knife to make the pumpkin features from the remaining black icing. Attach to the pumpkin with a little water. Secure the witch on the top of the cake with royal icing and arrange her accoutrements around the base.

Bluebird Bon Voyage Cake

This cake with its marble-effect sky, is sure to see someone off on an exciting journey in a very special way.

Serves 12–15

INGREDIENTS
1 x quantity Royal Icing
blue food colouring
2½ x quantity Sugarpaste Icing
1 x quantity Madeira Cake, baked in a
    20 cm/8 in round tin
1 x quantity Butter Icing
45 ml/3 tbsp Apricot Glaze
edible silver balls
thin pale blue ribbon

1 Make two-thirds of the royal icing softer, to use for filling in. Make the rest stiffer for the outlines and further piping. Tint the softer icing bright blue. Cover and leave overnight.

2 Make two different-size bird templates, and use to draw four large and five small birds onto greaseproof paper. Turn the paper over. Using a No 1 writing nozzle and white icing, pipe the outlines, and then fill in with blue icing. Leave to dry for at least 2 days.

3 Tint two-thirds of the sugarpaste icing blue. Form all the icing into small rolls and place them alternately together on a work surface. Form into a round and lightly knead to marble.

4 Cut the cake horizontally into three and sandwich together with the butter icing. Brush with apricot glaze. Roll out the marbled icing and use to cover the cake and a board. Place the cake on the board, flush with the edge.

5 Using the No 1 writing nozzle and the stiffer royal icing, pipe a wavy line around the edge of the board. Position the balls evenly in the icing. Secure the birds to the cake with royal icing. Pipe beads of white icing for eyes and stick on a ball. Drape the ribbon between the beaks, securing with icing.

COOK'S TIP: The finished cake can be kept for up to 1 week in an airtight container.

Christmas Stocking Cake

This charming rich fruit cake is easy to decorate in festive style.

Makes 1 x 20 cm/8 in square cake

INGREDIENTS
1 x 20 cm/8 in square
   Rich Fruit Cake
45 ml/3 tbsp Apricot Glaze
2 x quantity Marzipan
4 x quantity Sugarpaste Icing
15 ml/1 tbsp Royal Icing
red and green ribbons
red and green food colouring

1 Brush the cake with the apricot glaze and place on a 25 cm/10 in square cake board. Cover the cake with marzipan.

2 Set aside 225 g/8 oz/1½ cups of the sugarpaste icing. Cover the cake with the remainder and leave to dry. Secure the red ribbon around the board and the green ribbon around the cake with royal icing.

3 Divide the reserved sugarpaste icing in half and roll out one half. Using a template cut out two sugarpaste stockings, one 5 mm/¼ in larger all around. Put the smaller one on top of the larger one. Reserve the remaining white icing.

4 Divide the other half of the sugarpaste into two and tint one half red and the other green.

5 Roll out and cut seven 1 cm/½ in strips from each colour. Alternate the strips on top of the stocking. Roll lightly to fuse and press the edges together. Leave to dry.

6 Shape the remaining white sugarpaste into four parcels. Trim with red and green sugarpaste ribbons. Use the remaining red and green sugarpaste to make thin strips to decorate the cake sides. Secure in place with royal icing. Stick small sugarpaste balls over the joins. Arrange the stocking and parcels on the cake top.

Mouse in Bed

This cake is suitable for almost any age. Make the mouse well ahead to allow it time to dry.

Serves 8–10

INGREDIENTS
1 x quantity Quick-mix Sponge Cake, baked in a 20 cm/8 in square tin
⅓ x quantity Butter Icing
45 ml/3 tbsp Apricot Glaze
1 x quantity Marzipan
2 x quantity Sugarpaste Icing
blue and pink food colouring and pens

1 Cut 5 cm/2 in off one side of the cake. Split and fill the main cake with butter icing. Place on a cake board. With the cake off-cut, shape a hollowed pillow, the torso and the legs of the mouse. Brush the cake with apricot glaze and cover with marzipan. Cover the pillow and mouse's torso and legs in the same way. Leave to dry overnight.

2 Cover the cake and pillow with white sugarpaste icing. Lightly frill the edge of the pillow with a fork.

3 To make the valance, roll out 350 g/ 12 oz/2¼ cups of sugarpaste icing and cut into four 7.5 cm/3 in wide strips. Attach to the bed with water. Arrange the pillow and mouse's body on the cake.

4 For the quilt, tint 75 g/3 oz/½ cup of sugarpaste icing blue and roll out to an 18 cm/7 in square. Mark with a diamond pattern and with a flower cutter. Cover the mouse with the quilt.

5 Cut a 2.5 x 18 cm/1 x 7 in white sugarpaste icing strip for the sheet, mark the edge and place over the quilt, tucking it under at the top edge.

6 Tint 25 g/1 oz/2 tbsp of marzipan pink and make the head and paws of the mouse. Put the head on the pillow, tucked under the sheet, and the paws over the edge of the sheet. Use food colouring pens to draw on the face of the mouse.

Train Cake

This quick-and-easy train cake is made from a shaped tin, so all you need to do is decorate it!

Serves 8–10

INGREDIENTS

1½ x quantity Quick-mix Sponge Cake,
    baked in a train-shaped tin,
    about 35 cm/14 in long
2 x quantity Butter Icing
yellow food colouring
red liquorice bootlaces
90–120 ml/6–8 tbsp
    coloured vermicelli
4 liquorice wheels
pink and white cotton wool balls

1 Slice off the top surface of the cake to make it flat. Place diagonally on a cake board.

2 Tint the butter icing yellow. Use half of it to cover the cake.

COOK'S TIP: If you can't find a train shaped tin, cook the cake mix in a 23 cm/9 in square tin and cut out the shape.

3 Using a round nozzle and a quarter of the remaining butter icing, pipe a straight border around the top edge of the cake.

4 Place the red liquorice bootlaces on the piped border. Shape the bootlaces around the curves of the train to make a border. Pipe another butter-icing border inside the first border.

5 Using a small star nozzle and the remaining butter icing, pipe small stars over the top of the cake. Add extra liquorice and pipe other details, if you like. Use a palette knife to press on the coloured vermicelli all around the sides of the cake.

6 Press the liquorice wheels in place for the wheels of the train. Pull a couple of balls of cotton wool apart for the steam and stick onto the cake board with butter icing.

Number 7 Cake

Any combination of colours will work well for this marbled cake.

Serves 8–10

INGREDIENTS
1½ x quantity Quick-mix Sponge Cake,
    baked in 23 x 30 cm/9 x 12 in tin
1 x quantity orange-flavour Butter Icing
60 ml/4 tbsp Apricot Glaze
2 x quantity Sugarpaste Icing
blue and green food colouring
rice paper sweets

4 Immediately after covering, use a small "7" cutter to remove sugarpaste shapes in a random pattern from the covered cake.

1 Place the cake flat side up and cut out the number seven. Slice the cake horizontally, sandwich together with the butter icing and place on a board.

2 Brush the cake evenly with apricot glaze. Divide the sugarpaste icing into three and tint one of the pieces blue and another green. Set aside 50 g/ 2 oz/⅓ cup from each of the coloured icings.

3 Knead together the large pieces of blue and green icing with the third piece of white icing to marble. Use to cover the cake.

5 Roll out the reserved blue and green sugarpaste icing and stamp out shapes with the same cutter. Use these to fill the stamped-out shapes from the cake. Decorate the board with some rice paper sweets.

COOK'S TIP: If you are unsure about shaping the number seven cake freehand, you can purchase or hire shaped cake tins from specialist cake decorating shops.

Mermaid Cake

Pretty, elegant and flavoured with delicious chocolate, this cake must be every little girl's dream. The cake can be filled with butter icing.

Serves 6–8

INGREDIENTS
1 quantity chocolate-flavour Quick-mix
   Sponge Cake, baked in a
   900 g/2 lb loaf tin
450 g/1 lb plain chocolate
25 g/1 oz/3 cups
   unflavoured popcorn
1½ x quantity Sugarpaste Icing
lilac and pink
   food colouring
1 Barbie- or Sindy-type doll
45 ml/3 tbsp Apricot Glaze,
   plus a little extra
1 egg white, lightly beaten
demerara sugar
sea shells (optional)

1 Place the cake on a cake board. Melt the chocolate over a pan of simmering water. Stir in the popcorn until evenly coated, then spoon around the sides of the cake and on the board. Spread any remaining melted chocolate over the top of the cake.

2 Colour about three-quarters of the sugarpaste icing lilac and the remainder pink. Reserve the pink icing and one-third of the lilac icing wrapped in clear film. Roll out the remaining lilac icing to a rectangle wide enough to wrap around the doll's legs and about 5 cm/2 in longer.

3 Brush the doll from the waist down with the apricot glaze, then wrap her in the sugarpaste, lightly squeezing and pinching to make it stick. Pinch the end of the tail to form a fin shape, curling the ends slightly. Position the mermaid on the cake.

4 Roll out the remaining lilac and the pink sugarpaste icing and stamp out scales with a small crescent-shape cutter. Cover with clear film to prevent them from drying out. Starting at the fin, brush the crescents with a tiny amount of egg white and stick them to the tail, overlapping them, until it is completely covered.

Cut a shell-shaped bra top from the ~~t~~rimmings. Make indentations with the ~~ba~~ck of a knife and secure in place ~~w~~ith a little apricot glaze.

6 Scatter demerara sugar around the base of the cake for sand and add a few real shells, if you like. Remove the doll before serving.

57

Pizza Cake

Quick, easy and impressive – this deliciously sweet cake is a definite winner for pizza fanatics everywhere. Serve in small wedges.

Serves 8–10

INGREDIENTS
1 x quantity Quick-mix
    Sponge Cake,baked
    in a 23 cm/9 in shallow,
    round cake tin
1 x quantity Butter Icing
red, yellow and green
    food colouring
⅓ x quantity Marzipan
25 g/1 oz/2 tbsp Sugarpaste Icing
15 ml/1 tbsp desiccated coconut

1 Place the cake on a pizza plate. Colour the butter icing red and spread evenly over the top of the cake. Leave a 1 cm/½ in border around the edge of the cake.

2 Colour the marzipan yellow, if necessary, then coarsely grate it. Sprinkle over the red butter icing to represent cheese.

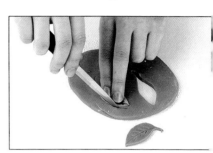

3 Colour the sugarpaste icing green. Roll out to about a 5 mm/¼ in thickness. Cut out two leaf shapes freehand or cut around a real leaf. Mark the veins with a knife and add to the pizza cake for the garnish.

4 Place the desiccated coconut in a small bowl and colour with green food colouring. Scatter over the pizza cake to represent chopped herbs.

COOK'S TIP: The finished cake can be kept in the fridge for up to 1 week.

Ladybird Cake

Children will love this colourful and appealing ladybird, and it is very
simple to make.

Serves 10–12

INGREDIENTS
1½ x quantity Quick-mix
   Sponge Cake, baked in a
   1.2 litre/2 pint/5 cup
   pudding bowl
½ x quantity Butter Icing
60 ml/4 tbsp lemon curd, warmed
3 x quantity Sugarpaste Icing
red, black and green food colouring
5 marshmallows
50 g/2 oz/4 tbsp Marzipan
2 pipe cleaners

1 Cut the cake in half horizontally
and sandwich together with the butter
icing. Cut vertically through the cake,
about a third of the way in. Brush
both pieces with the lemon curd.
Colour 450 g/1 lb/3 cups of the
sugarpaste icing red. Roll out to
5 mm/¼ in thick and cover the larger
piece of cake to make the body. Using
a skewer, make an indentation down
the centre for the wings.

2 Colour 350 g/12 oz/2¼ cups of the
icing black, roll out three-quarters and
use to cover the smaller piece of cake
for the head. Place both cakes on a
cakeboard, press together.

3 Roll out 50 g/2 oz/⅓ cup of icing
and cut out two 5 cm/2 in rounds for
the eyes, then stick to the head with
water. Roll out the remaining black
icing and cut out eight 4 cm/1½ in
rounds. Use two of these for the eyes
and stick the others on to the body.

4 Place the ladybird on a cake board.
Colour some icing green and squeeze
through a garlic crusher to make grass.
Flatten the marshmallows, snip and
stick a marzipan round in the centre of
each. Colour pipe cleaners black and
press a ball of black icing on to the
end of each. Arrange the grass and
flowers around the ladybird. If you
have sufficient trimmings, make baby
ladybirds as well, if you like.

Banjo Cake

The perfect cake for a musical child. It can be set on a large tray or you could cut out a card template to support it.

Serves 15–20

INGREDIENTS

2 x quantity Quick-mix Sponge Cake,
    baked in one 20 cm/8 in round tin and one
    18 cm/7 in square tin
115 g/4 oz/6 tbsp seedless raspberry
    jam, warmed
2⅔ x quantity Sugarpaste Icing
lime green food colouring
2 coloured sticks of liquorice
4 round lollipops
60 ml/4 tbsp coloured vermicelli
pieces of flat green liquorice
2 long red liquorice bootlaces
4 long green liquorice bootlaces
ribbon and 2 pins, for the strap
Sugarpaste stars (optional)

1 Cut the dome off the round cake and place bottom side up. Cut the dome off the square cake, then cut in half down the middle. Place together in a banjo shape. Draw round them on stiff card and cut out to make a reinforcing template.

2 Stamp out a shallow hole in the round cake with a 5 cm/2 in cutter. Place the cakes on the base and brush with the jam.

3 Colour the sugarpaste icing lime green and roll out to a 62 x 25 cm/ 25 x 10 in rectangle. Cover the banjo easing the icing into the hollow and down the sides. Make finger indentations along the length of the neck on each side.

4 Cut off four 1 cm/½ in pieces from 1 liquorice stick and press into the top end of the banjo neck. Place the remaining piece and the other liquorice stick next to the hollow. Dip the lollipops in water and then in the coloured vermicelli. Press them into the sides of the neck end to line up with the liquorice.

5 Place the flat liquorice pieces side by side at the base, securing with a little water. Cut the red bootlace into 5 cm/2 in lengths. Position them along the neck to make frets, securing with water if necessary.

COOK'S TIP: The finished cake can be made up to 2 days in advance and kept in a cool, dry place.

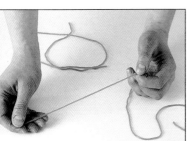

6 Dip the green bootlaces in hot water and stretch until straight. Wrap one end of the bootlace strings around the liquorice sticks and attach the other ends to the flat liquorice pieces. Secure the ribbon strap with pins and decorate the banjo with sugarpaste stars, if wished. **Do not forget to remove the pins before serving.**

Index

This edition published by Hermes House

Hermes House is an imprint of
Anness Publishing Limited
Hermes House, 88–89 Blackfriars Road, London SE1 8HA

Publisher: Joanna Lorenz
Editor: Valerie Ferguson
Series Designer: Bobbie Colgate Stone
Designer: Andrew Heath
Reader: Diane Ashmore
Production Controller: Joanna King

Recipes contributed by: Patricia Lousada, Sue Maggs,
Sarah Maxwell, Janice Murfitt, Angela Nilson,
Louise Pickford.

Photography: Edward Allwright, David Armstrong,
Amanda Heywood, Tim Hill.

Notes:
For all recipes, quantities are given in both metric
imperial measures and, where appropriate, measu
are also given in standard cups and spoons.
Follow one set, but not a mixture, because they
not interchangeable.

Standard spoon and cup measures are level.

1 tsp = 5 ml   1 tbsp =15 ml

1 cup = 250 ml/8 fl oz

Australian standard tablespoons are 20 ml.
Australian readers should use 3 tsp in place of 1
for measuring small quantities of gelatine, cornflo
salt, etc.

Medium eggs are used unless otherwise statec

Printed and bound in China

© Anness Publishing Limited 1999, updated 2000
2 3 4 5 6 7 8 9 10